Dinosaur Publications

The Stock Exchange

by Althea

illustrated by Chris Evans

Published by Dinosaur Publications Ltd, Over, Cambridge, Great Britain.
for the Council of The Stock Exchange in Great Britain and Ireland

ISBN 0/85122/322–2 (paperback)
ISBN 0/85122/323–0 (hardback)
Made in Great Britain

In the past, when groups of people met in London coffee houses, they sometimes decided to put their money together to buy ships.

They sent the ships around the world to trade with other countries.

If a ship was successful and made money out of buying goods and selling them to other countries, the profits were shared out.
Each person would get a share of the profit according to the share of the money he had put towards buying the ship.

Many of these voyages took a long time – sometimes years – and while the ship was away some of the merchants might need their money back to spend on something else. They would go to one of the coffee houses to see if anybody wanted to buy their share of the ship. Later, other businesses all over the country were financed in the same way: mines, factories, canals, and so on.

In 1773 the merchants decided they needed their own place to do all the buying and selling of their shares in these businesses, so they started The Stock Exchange.

Today the Exchange is still the place where people who want to buy or sell stocks and shares can meet.

If someone has some savings or spare money
which she wants to grow, she might ask
a stockbroker to buy shares in a company for her.

This means she has a share
in everything the company owns.
The company pays her a share of the profit
it makes, because she owns some of that too.
This is called a dividend.

Later, if she needs her money back –
perhaps to help pay for a new home –
she asks her stockbroker
to sell the shares to someone else.
Her stockbroker will also advise on many other
financial matters, such as tax and insurance.

SHARE PRICES
B.P.
JOHN LEWIS
MARKS & SPENCER
BRITISH OXYGEN

Many people's savings are used to buy
stocks and shares through The Stock Exchange,
often without the people knowing!
They may belong to a pension fund,
whose money is invested through
The Stock Exchange to make it grow
and so provide pensions for retired people.
Trade Unions invest some of their
members' money on The Stock Exchange.

Lots of people have a life assurance policy
and pay a small sum of money every month.
Together this adds up to a large amount.
Some of that money is invested on The Stock Exchange
and will be used to provide the payments which
the Insurance Company has to make when
people retire or die.

CADBURY
SCHWEPPES

A company may need extra money
to build a new factory or pay for new machines
or maybe to invent new things to sell.
It can get this money by selling new shares
through The Stock Exchange.

The people who buy these shares hope
that the company will become
more profitable and that their shares
will be worth more money.

SHELL

The Government borrows lots of money
through The Stock Exchange
to build new schools, hospitals and roads
and to help pay for many other things.
People lend their money to the Government
and they are paid interest regularly in return.

The Stock Exchange is run by a Council voted for by the Members of The Stock Exchange. The Members all have to obey very strict rules and regulations so that everybody's savings are safely looked after.

There are other Stock Exchange trading floors
in different parts of the country.
They all work closely together
to the same rules.

It is important that all investors have
the same information about the companies
so that nobody has an unfair advantage.

If a company has made large profits or losses,
the price of its shares may change.
This news must be kept secret
until everybody can be told at the same time.
This secret news is sent from London
by computer to the other trading floors.

by Anna Ragon

coivent, relativement aux rimes, n'est que celle des rimes elles-mêmes. une s'explique par l'autre, il n'est pas besoin de revenir sur ce sujet fisamment développé dans le chapitre précédent. Les qualificatifs r lesquels on désigne les rimes s'appliquent aussi aux vers : vers *sculins*, vers *féminins*, vers *suivis*, vers *croisés*, vers *embrassés*, vers *lés*, etc. Divers exemples en ont été donnés plus haut (p. 54 et 55).

disposition des vers, quant aux mesures, est de deux sortes : l'une ils ont le même nombre de pieds, et l'autre où ils ne l'ont pas; voici huitain du type vers *embrassés à disposition alternée* du poète temporain Jacques Carton, intitulé *l'Appel* :

Menace de velours, sphère aux absurdes bords,
Abysses inversés où je glisse, où je tombe;
Air des nuits, vieux soupir qu'échangent Ciel et Tombe
Et toi, silence, ô chœur inouï d'outre-accords!

Versez-nous l'infini, inexhaustibles urnes.
Que ce lait d'astres bleus nous rende un cœur d'enfant,
Même si traîne encor, tel d'un vain olifant,
L'appel des mondes morts par les cimes nocturnes.

un morceau contenant des vers de douze et de huit syllabes *mêlés*, s gracieux, de La Fontaine :

COMPANY ANNOUNCEMENTS
FISONS
WOOLWORTHS
MOTHERCARE
ICI

When a new company wants to raise money through The Stock Exchange the staff at the Exchange carefully study the company's accounts. They see what the company is doing and how it spends its money.

They also find out about the people who run the company and make sure they are honest and sensible.

A company whose shares are listed on The Stock Exchange will have to obey the rules and regulations which make sure that it is run properly.

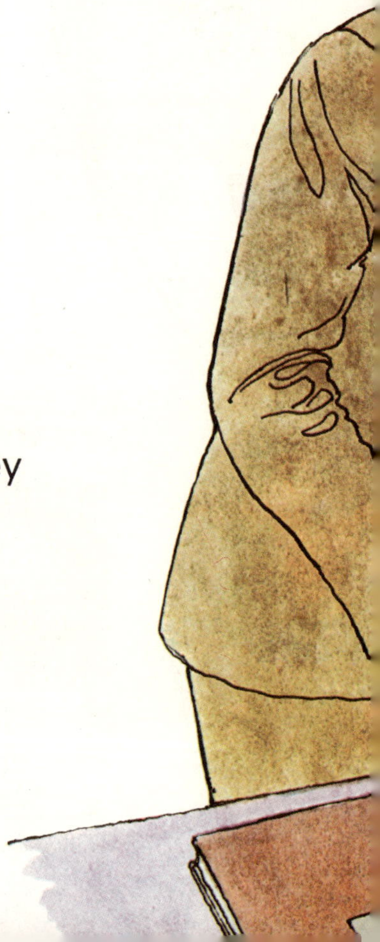

Each morning The Stock Exchange
is opened by the ringing of a bell.
The trading floor is a big market place.
The traders are called jobbers
and their market stalls are called pitches.
They try to make a profit by buying shares
and selling them for more money.

Lots of jobbers are buying
and selling the same shares
in competition with each other.
It is like a market where lots of stallholders
may sell the same sort of oranges
at slightly different prices.

The stockbrokers are the customers.
They come to the market to buy or sell
shares for the investors.

Before telling a jobber
whether he wants to buy or sell,
the broker will ask the price of the shares.
The jobber gives a buying price and
a selling price.

The broker then goes round the market
asking other jobbers for their prices.
He soon sees where he can buy the shares
for the least money or sell them for the most.

The broker goes back to deal with
the jobber who offers the best bargain.
The jobber and the broker each writes
the details in his own notebook.
The deal is done.

The actual transfer of the shares
to the new owners is done later in the offices
and then the money will be paid.
Accounting and paperwork
is mostly done by computer
and this makes things much easier.

At the end of each day's trading
a waiter sounds a rattle.
This means the market is closed.

The Stock Exchange helps the Government
to borrow the money it needs
to run the country.
Companies can get money
to help them make and sell more goods.
They hope this will increase their profits.
Part of these profits are paid as dividends to the investors.
Some is paid as tax to the Government,
which uses this money to help run the country.
Money left over is kept in the company
to pay for new factories, new machinery,
and the other expenses of running and
developing the business.

People who save money for the future
can invest it and earn extra money.
They also know they can get their savings
back quickly when they need the money.

DEBENHAMS

Glossary

Bear	Someone who thinks prices will go down.
Broker	The Stockbroker (or 'broker') is the person who buys or sells shares for a customer.
Bull	Someone who thinks prices will go up.
Dividend	Part of a company's profit paid to shareholders – usually twice a year.
Interest	Money paid for the use of money borrowed.
Investor	The saver or organisation which buys stocks and shares.
Jobber	A Jobber trades in shares, buying or selling them to brokers.
Pension Fund	A fund into which people put part of their pay. It gives them a pension when they stop working.

Shares	People pay money to the company and in return get a share in the company, so shareholders are the real owners. They hold regular meetings to hear how the company is being run.
Stag	Someone who buys shares in a new company hoping that when they are first resold on The Stock Exchange the price will go up and he will make a profit.
Stocks	Another word for shares, also Government and other loans on which investors receive interest.
Trading Floor	The market place of The Stock Exchange where shares are bought and sold.
Waiter	Someone employed to help on the floor of The Stock Exchange taking messages etc. Called a waiter because long ago, the waiters in the coffee houses used to take messages.

You can arrange to visit your nearest Stock Exchange to see it all working and find out more for yourself.

The Stock Exchange, London